Published in 2017 by Happy Planet Creative Arts CIC

British Library Cataloguing in Publication Data:
A catalogue record for this book is available from the British Library.

ISBN: 9780956039255

Happy Planet Creative Arts CIC

3A Ilfracombe Gardens

Whitley Bay

NE26 3ND

Lines From
An Unfinished Love Song

A journey in poetry

Gail Curry

"Throw your dreams into space like a kite,
and you do not know what it will bring back,
a new life, a new friend, a new love, a new country."

Anais Nin

Contents

Grief, Depression and PTSD

Introduction

I met Yelena (Lena) for the first time on October 30th 2000 in Warsaw. I had instant curiosity for the woman who had been brought up in a closed Soviet city and lived a life determined by the state, not of her choosing. The reality of this meant that she had spent her life as a member of the armed forces but in her heart she was an artist of distinctive talent. She eventually showed herself to be an eloquent and generous friend, with an unquenchable thirst for knowledge of the world outside of Russia, as well as an equally astounding knowledge of what lay within it, especially her beloved Siberia.

We met at the same birthday each year over the course of a weekend on three more occasions before Lena asked me to be her pen pal, which I agreed to do. We corresponded via clandestine methods and met at the birthday each year, where eventually I spoke of my long standing wish to see the real Russia. Lena offered to be my guide immediately, although added that she was unsure when it would be possible.

Finally in 2010 I was shown the Russia seldom seen by tourists, the one Lena knew intimately. That journey irreparably changed the path of our lives. I returned home in February after a month with Lena and felt completely bereft when only halfway home. I knew falling in love with her created what at first appeared to be an impossible situation, given the complexities of the politics and everything that entailed. What I didn't know immediately was that she felt the same. I returned to visit Lena in May of the same year and over time we solved the issues by making the decision to start a new life elsewhere, which brought another set of problems we addressed together. We married secretly on New Year's Eve 2012. Sadly Lena was killed in December 2013, four months before she was due to leave Russia, while trying to rescue others from a landslide she had survived in the Western Caucasus mountains.

As with so many areas of our lives that were very different but could be seen in parallel, her death signalled a series of events in mine that led me into the darkest of times. Only weeks after Lena's death my home was burgled in the early hours of the morning by two men, who I woke to find in my bedroom. This event triggered the re-emergence of an event earlier in my life, a violent corrective rape at the age of 17 by a group of men, which I had buried psychologically in order to survive. The combination of those events triggered the beginning of the perfect storm of Post-Traumatic Stress Disorder (PTSD).

The story of our lives is for a different book, but here I am sharing a selection of the poems I wrote and read to Lena, with her comments in places, as well as those I offered to her through the universe after her death. The remaining poems represent my personal journey through grief, depression and PTSD, the contemplation of suicide, finally finding the light of acceptance and recovery after what was a very dark and lonely journey.

My encounters with NHS mental health services were for the most part unhelpful, disempowering and lacked compassion. I was completely unprepared for the way I would be treated and the attitudes I would encounter, having spent a large part of my working life in social care before I became an artist. While it is undeniable the NHS is under-funded and resourced, it is my assertion that is no excuse for a lack of compassion, blaming and shaming attitudes or blatant abuse of policies, some of which were unfit for purpose.

I pursued two formal complaints against Northumbria Healthcare NHS Foundation Trust and Northumberland Tyne & Wear NHS Foundation Trust, as well as a formal complaint that has been passed to the Parliamentary Ombudsman against Northumbria Healthcare NHS Foundation Trust, all with the help of North East NHS Independent Complaints Advocacy. This was both time-consuming and energy sapping, but I felt it necessary to obtain the treatment I needed. My quest for appropriate treatment began in October 2014, but I didn't receive it until October 2016. I have no doubt in my mind that had I not undertaken the complaints I did and insisted on my rights I would not be recovering or have received EMDR treatment, which has begun to transform my life. I have three pieces of advice for anyone finding themselves in a similar position: 1) Get an advocate. 2) Get an advocate. 3) Get an advocate.

In sharing my verses I want to offer some light and hope to those who feel they have none. Please do not give up, I almost did, but I am so glad I decided not to, our lives are worth fighting for.

Be brave my friend, you will complete your journey too, it just takes longer than we would wish.

Gail Curry
July 2017

Friendship
&
Love

Time travelling

Through the pictures and the artifacts
the sculptures and the tomes
hand in hand
through the centuries we roam.
From revolution to devolution
Tudor courts to civil wars
Romantic poets and revolving doors.
Everything changing, but one constant
that is us, hand in hand
on this uncharted journey.

This was the first poem I wrote to Lena in 2004, she loved hearing about my travels in my letters to her. When she had leave from the army she would pick up my letters from her aunt on her way home, together with some chocolate, then she would immerse herself in the accounts of my travels. Her favourites were always the museums and galleries, which I knew to describe in great detail for her. Lena had no internet access, so I became her version of Google.

Sandcastles on Sunday

Gritty, golden, cold
but fun to mould.
Myriad of ages washed and worn
grains of history between my toes
journeying on tides from distant lands
to build sandcastles on a Sunday.

In a letter from 2005 Lena asked me where my favourite place was, so I told her about Holy Island in Northumberland. I described it as, 'A tiny magical island that the sea wraps itself around and only allows mortals on for a few hours each day. Mermaids sing, birds dance in the wind and time stands still on golden dunes of ancient sand, while children build sandcastles to feed their imagination.' When she replied she said she'd like to visit but wanted to know what a sandcastle was, I drew a picture and wrote the poem. We spoke of the island often, I described it as my spiritual home. Lena became enchanted with it and hoped one day that we would visit it together.

Others

Let others lead small lives, but not you.
Let others argue over small things, but not you.
Let others cry over small hurts, but not you.
Let others leave their future in someone else's hands, but not you.
Visit all the places you yearn to see, be free.
Become all you wish and more.
Shine like the brightest star in the night sky every single day.

Lena seemed very depressed. She was struggling with being stationed with people who she had nothing in common with. To make matters worse the garrison was over 300 miles from the nearest town, so opportunities for 'a change of scene' were non-existent. I did my best to remind her that change would come. When I wrote of how to meditate, she wrote back three months later to thank me, she wished she could spend the next two years in that state.

Running towards freedom

Feet cushioned for the journey
body sleekly wrapped
route and destination unknown.
Freedom beckons me to run towards her.
The early steps jolt my body, until I find my feet.
I am sluggish and uncoordinated
my senses neither fully tuned or relaxed.

Each step awakens them from their slumber in mundane captivity.
I feel the coldness of the wind licking my legs
usually cosseted by the restrictions of conformity.
As I push through the air to freedom
it forces itself upon my face
taunting me with the smell and taste of it.
Reassuringly alive and waking with each stride
I am hungry for the taste and fulfillment.

Free from responsibility
my body finds its natural rhythm with each step to move unhindered
I dare to leave it to its own devices.
Arriving at the junction should I admire the view
or spring clean my mind?
The signpost says freedom in both directions
so it's a free choice.
Banana skins, dog poo and Ipod wearing cyclists pepper my path.

As I turn left the ground rises to meet me.
I feel the gradient on my throat and in my lungs
but the dogs of cold air have left my legs now.
Beads of sweat form on me, they draw out the clutter of the day
amassed in my mind.
Some collect and form little streams
which slalom down my face to my chin
where the wind of freedom encourages them to jump like lemmings.

My lungs are pumping freedom through my veins
my legs and arms work in unison and harmony to aid them.
I can hear my heartbeat; my pulse throb
my feet crushing fallen leaves
or momentarily suffocating the grass.
I feel the fires of freedom scorch my throat and burn in my chest
as I plunder puddles with my fast moving feet.

I could stop
but the feeling of freedom is stronger than the aching in my limbs.
I set myself a target
the top of that hill where the sun rests now.
I could be Icarus flying
a fox evading hounds
but I am Mercury with winged heels
for now I am free.

Lena decided she would run a marathon in 2009, partly to break the boredom of her days, to raise morale among her troops and to challenge herself. She knew there was no point challenging me to run, 'more likely I see a whale flying,' she laughed. She wasn't wrong. However she did challenge me to write her a poem about running. This was the first of such challenges she set, 'to keep me out of mischief.' Lena did complete her marathon, she loved this poem and the stories of Icarus and Mercury I shared with her.

Curious, so curious

I like to sit and ponder
on such things as navel fluff
of honey bees and boney knees
the real important stuff.

I wonder why it is the sky
is never upside down
or when a crocodile is sad
can it ever frown?

Are roses with an attitude
the kind we know as prim
and are cigars that diet
known as Panatella Slims?

Do toads play chess on Saturdays
and do they use frogs pawns?
When bubbles burst are witches cursed
to sunbathe on the lawn?

If willows weep do ashes burn
when cricketers get out?
But most of all I'd like to know
What men are all about?

Lena loved language and learning new words, so I thought I would test her a little. She wrote in 2005, 'I do not fully understand this, will you tell me when we meet next please, the poem and men.'

Poetry of the metronome

Poetry by numbers, ten beats per line
The words must flow like music, keep in time.
But mine are like jazz, all over the place
they can't keep the sonnet form, but race on
feel constricted as they try to leave
struggle from beneath the pillow to breathe.
I must fight my emotions, play a part
for poems aren't simply songs from the heart.
There's structure and order, rules to obey
you can't just put down what you want to say.
Form must be kept to, or where would we be?
Poetically tuned anarchy.

Poetry by numbers, ten beats per line
maybe I'll rebel today and write just nine.

Lena referred to me in a letter of 2007 as 'the happy rebel.' She asked for a poem of rebellion, I gave her this. She told me she was disappointed, she expected a revolution. I told her they took longer to plan than a week.

Chocolate – the curse of the brown bean

If you were a chocolate
what kind would you be?
How would you be wrapped and packed
apart from tastefully?

Would you be a Hero
who lived on Quality Street?
Or Mars en route to the Milky Way perhaps
passing through a Galaxy.

Would you be a Drifter
stopping for the occasional Picnic?
Or a Lion, bar none, watching from a Double Decker
Flaked out.

Oh my taste buds tingle
all this talk of choc
I need Time Out, for a break
for a Kit-Kat
I have the Munchies.

Most days I can wait until After Eight
before I am seduced by the brown bean.
I close my eyes and imagine being serenaded
by wandering Minstrels
as they melt upon my tongue.

Or perhaps the mysterious Milk Tray woman
will cast her Black Magic as I sleep.
I am no friend of the Milky Bar kid
his blondeness doesn't fool me
not enough cocoa and far too sugary.

I prefer the deep intensity
of good old Green & Blacks
it really hits that certain spot
that others often lack.

Not that I'm a chocolate snob
I cannot be restricted
to the brown bean I am always drawn
and beautifully addicted.

This was a challenge poem. Lena had a very sweet tooth and loved chocolate. I mused that she was addicted, she didn't disagree.

Looking up at the night sky

I look up at the night sky
and gaze at the beauty above.
My eyes are transfixed to the shining white light
metallic blue twinkle of Orion
all on the backdrop of the majestic dark canvas.
I begin to stare as deep as I can into the universe
and feel not small and insignificant
as once thought in the past
but being part of something so spectacular.
Standing in time.

As I stand here now I see a million years past.
Time travelling
as what I see now is so old
but so new to my eyes.
What there is now
may no longer exist
a galactic sum of stars
motionless in and around
the dark heavenly void.
So often unnoticed
yet so chaotic, still has me in awe
transported into the deep beauty
true and simple
yet such intense splendour.

I wrote this after a visit to Norway in 2008 to see the Northern Lights, which failed to appear. Lena wrote, 'I know of better skies, I know of deeper skies, limitless skies, I will show you Siberian skies, where spirits soar and ancestors guard the earth.' She did too and it was every bit as magical as she foretold.

January journey

Far behind me now and out of sight
is the glow of Christmas and New Year.
Grey and sombre are the days and at night
the deadly biting frosts come prowling near
like arctic wolves, breathing winter kill.

But we are cheerful and of good resolve
on the whole
and set about our journey with a will
hoping our misgivings will dissolve
in sunny days and peaceful times ahead.

May good fortune take us as a friend
as we in expectation gladly tread
the road that leads us to the year's unknown end
attempting to embrace every moment for its sake
awake at every new step we take.

This poem marked the beginning of our month long journey of discovery through Russia by train. Every stop a new experience and a new challenge for one or both of us.

Beautiful brown eyes

Your face, dripping with the dew of youth.
Your eyes, bottomless pools of such brown depth
that plead to be explored and gazed upon.
Your hopes and dreams reflected in them
take heart and hold fast, know you are loved
just like HP sauce.

Lena loved this little verse. She had no idea what HP sauce was, but enjoyed the joke when I explained. Her code for 'I love you' in later letters was 'HP.'

Morning meadow thoughts

Roaming in the meadows
in the early morning dew
breathing deep the fragrant air
and my thoughts go out to you.

In confines of the city
with its murk and shadows grey
and I would that you were here with me
to greet this splendid day.

High above the lark is singing
while the sky is changing hue
as the sun comes forth in glory
bringing distant hills in view.

But of you I can't help thinking
in that distant sombre land
wishing you were here with me
in these meadows, hand in hand.

This was the last poem I wrote to Lena as her pen pal. I had returned home from our trip and I realised I was in love with her and missed her terribly.

By night

I came alone on the road by night.
In scented darkness, I knocked before the light.
Your face, pale, serene, the moon of all my dreams
bestowed lustres of pearl, whose scattered gleams
shone in our touching eyes; yours brown, mine blue
me blushing on the brink of your gateway.

Conquering brightness, your dawn in my dark
signing my heart with your most secret mark
placed with a kiss, flowering scarlet sweet
reddened within, hidden, closed and complete.

The azure of first light, gold in your hair
makes lucid your invitations to share
those radiant roses of delicate snow petalled silk
kissed by the risen sun's glow.
Drawn by your gold, to the home whence it flowed
I came alone by night, down a very long road.

Fortunately when I returned to Siberia in May of the same year I found that Lena felt just as I did. This was the beginning of finding solutions to problems we felt were insurmountable. Thankfully we found our way down a very long road.

I think of you and smile

I think of you and smile
and in that moment of warm tenderness
I feel you wander barefoot through my days and senses.
Your footsteps are gentle and warm
they tickle me with your humour and mischief.
No matter what my mood
I feel those long affectionate arms
sometimes a warm loving embrace
soft and endless like the heat of the morning sun.
Occasionally it's more passionate
as your hands trace my silhouette
like the flames of a fire.

Writing love letters and poems to the person who illuminates your world is one of life's pleasures in my opinion. One really shouldn't have to write them through a third party, but that is what we had to do, as Lena would have been guilty of the equivalent of treason had our relationship been discovered. It was a complex clandestine process involving translation as well as ensuring a list of certain words were not used for fear of them falling into the wrong hands. I am truly grateful to Anya Klovochesky, the best friend anyone could wish for, who translated tirelessly in both directions and never once poked fun or commented on the contents.

The secret garden

Even now, I see your calm, trustful face.
I seem to hear you breathing as you talk of long days
warm nights and a secret place
which you found, by chance, on a summer walk.
I asked you to take me to that garden.
You shook your pale hair down, went on smiling
your body did not resist or harden when I came close
but still you said nothing.
I wrapped up your gentle warmth in my arms
confiding and kind, you kept your silence.
As we found a peace free from all alarm
you soothed me with the touch of your patience.
Having filled me with your calm, you hugged me
whispering words which blossomed, secretly.

Lena's home was a very old log cabin several miles from the city of her birth. It was her sanctuary, built by her family surrounded by woods and orchards planted by them over generations. It was within that space alone, her secret garden, she could be her authentic self, luminous and enchanting.

Sex & chocolate

Flowing over me
a river of warm silk
your breath like candle flame
your lips softly tempting like Haagen-Dazs
your smile.

Your skin
soft and smooth as chocolate
when I bite, a sea of sugar hits my lips
I taste sweet waves of pleasure.

When you touch and kiss me
there are no similes.

Lena's response to this poem: 'I can not look at chocolate without having impure thoughts now, you have corrupted me, just as the Party warned.' My response, 'Mission accomplished.'

I see you

I look at you and what do I see, in your photograph and in my mind? I see you; strong, imperfect, but beautiful like a kaleidoscope to a child's eye. A mixture of so many colours; shapes and lights, all dancing with each other.

I see your smile; it is the essence of you and shows itself in so many different forms. It welcomes me into your eyes; they are dark but glisten, cavernous yet tempting, so hypnotic and alluring. They invite me into the vast warm space that is you, to swim weightless.

As I bathe in you; your arms are never far away, I sense them, waiting, waiting for that moment, to take me, to hold me, tenderly, lovingly, when I need swim alone no longer.

Your mouth displays the physical smile, the sign of happiness, on gentle, firm, feminine lips. It delivers the words from deep within. Sometimes the flow is truncated, when you are uncertain of the audience, or your confidence deserts you, but when the flow returns it is soft on the ear like velvet, ever pure like moonlight, ever true like the beat of a heart, your heart.

Your words wash over me, but not all, some penetrate my skin and deeper. They are potent and luminous, reading them injects me with a glistening joy that could so easily intoxicate me, but I am neither blinded or lose myself, I know you would not want that for me. Instead they warm me, illuminate the shadows, draw me ever closer.

Closer to your body, that warm soft temptation that represents you physically. Those strong yet gentle arms I dream of, during waking hours or sleep. Your body is beautiful, not because it is taut and toned though efforts, exertions and physical trials, but because it is a part of you, your embodiment. Scarred with the past, in the past, decorated with your tattooed self-expressions, womanly and feminine it remains, striking in its silhouette and seductive sensuality. The curves and contours guide my eye softly from your cheekbones, to your chin both strong and characterful.

Your neck holds your head proudly and justifiably, your shoulders display your resilience and determination, they would shelter anyone well.

Your torso and back tantalise me like chocolate, warm and richly sensual, they beckon my attention, to touch, caress and ultimately taste and savour them.

And finally your legs, the means of your movement and your stability, they have carried you this far, so they are reliable and robust, but I know there is more, as they appear to be endless.

There is more inside you. I feel your strength and your wisdom; they grow in your secret garden with so many other qualities. You tend them when no one is looking, but I watch secretly though the hole in the fence, your defence.

I see you smile as your garden flowers and grows; as you care for it, nurture it, protect it, as the old walled garden is no more. Sometimes you sit in it, you watch the clouds, or lie on the grass smiling while picking daisies, the sun shines on you and the butterflies play, as the birds sing.

What was once a walled garden is no more. There is a softer landscape created in the light of experience; by a woman of vision and direction, one who is not afraid of toil or change, one who can dream and can equally face challenge. The seeds are sown; tend them just as before, be brave and share your garden, show yourself and your boundless beauty.

I wrote this for Lena when she was having a very difficult time at work dealing with being responsible for disciplining others for being gay. Her sense of self suffered badly, she felt I would tire of waiting for her. I needed to convince her she was wrong and I loved her unconditionally. She asked me what I saw in her, so I told her with this piece of prose.

At a loss for words

A hundred thousand words or more
and yet I am mute!
Unable to articulate
or enunciate the prose inside.

A million words or more perhaps
Yet I am dumb!
My mind filled with a fog that will not clear
as I search desperately for my vernacular.

My lexical knowledge has left me
my diction has all but departed
speechless I am!
Whilst letters run past me – teasing.

If I could just catch a word
maybe a passage would follow
but I fear my subconscious protects me
from the torrent that would be unleashed.

So if you want to know how I am feeling
then you will have to come closer to see
hold me close, look deep into my eyes
and break the silence.

Watching Lena paint was one of my greatest pleasures. I tried several times to write a poem about it, but words were insufficient to capture all she became in that pursuit. She would fasten up her long hair by fixing it in place with pencils, take a coffee to her easel and begin the magic. She moved effortlessly, fluidly in her own blissful zone, singing to herself, completely unaware of anything outside of herself and the canvas. I watched for hours at a time, I never tired of it, as painting was her joy.

Casting your net

Hands placed behind your back
your head bowed down
you rise slowly to catch your prey.

Catching my gaze and holding it intently
your eyes pierce deep inside of me
I give in willingly
to see where you will lead me.

Lost completely
in the music, in the moment
in you
there is nothing else.

You dance slowly towards me
pushing me back without touching me
then you withdraw and I am drawn with you
attached by an invisible thread.

Back, forth
round again
never losing my gaze
my attention total.

The rhythm is hypnotic
like you
your eyes
your moving body.

Stop! I say.
You release me with a knowing smile
You know you will catch me again.

Lena only had to smile and peer over her glasses at me and I was immersed in contentment. She would ask why I was smiling, each time I would reply, 'because you love me and that is all I need.' She blushed every time.

I want you

I want your hand in mine
to feel you close
to guide me
when I am in danger of losing my way.

I need your shoulder to rest my head upon
your arms to hold me safely
to chase the ghosts that don't belong
but haunt me, in life and in dreams.

I want you to speak to me as you would be spoken to
listen to me like a friend
see me as an equal
and touch me like a lover.

I want you to let my hair down
to remind me I am alive
that I am capable of love
both in the present and the future.

I want you in my dreams
whether for a fleeting visit on a magic carpet
or to stay with me by a fire
until we wake.

I want your lips on my lips
to taste your soft mouth
that speaks the words
that gently kiss my very being.

I want your warm body against mine
to undress you, to caress you
to listen to your heart beat
to hear you breathe in the moonlight.

I want you next to me
in me, around me
to share thoughts, passions and desires
to be the blanket for my bones.

I want to look into your eyes
and whisper in your ear
as your body rises and falls
in the rhythm of love.

I want your breath on my skin
your hands on my body
to give your eyes sight into my heart
my soul, my very being
I want you.

Lena's response in a letter dated 2012, 'Your words bring spring early to this quiet Siberian heart, it blossoms only for you.'

Winter passions

The gilt of candlelight on yellow pine
swept your shoulders with gleams of softened gold.
Intimately sheltered from the wind's whine
our shy affection began to unfold.
The stars sealed the ocean of black heaven.
The moon rolled her silver above our lair.
The snow fields were naked, wild and windspun
their slopes undulating with brazen flair.
The long night unravelled our reticence.
Safely cloaked by her kindly discretion
time stripped the remains of our ignorance
granting our attraction its conclusion.
The crowning of love by tender actions
was fulfillment for our winter passions.

Although I work as an artist I didn't consider myself a painter. Lena disagreed. She wrote in 2013, 'Do not tell me you do not paint. You might not use a brush but your pen makes landscapes and portraits with words deeper than paint could ever reach.'

Sunrise

Through the velvety layers of waking
the newly risen sun, warm on my back
opening my eyes to a gentle cloud of thoughts
and the sleeping form of my sweetheart.

Her face is at rest, breathing softly
beautiful and stroked with sunlight
golden hair rests on her sensitive skin
cocooned in the duvet, with my hopes and dreams.

Starting each day with such a vision
lavishly fills my heart with sweet tenderness
makes still my soul without want or need
except to wake with her
to share each new day.

This was the final poem I wrote and read to Lena in person, in August 2013. We knew we would part soon and not see one another for many months with all communications ceasing because of her new posting. Lena put on a brave face and told me it would pass quickly and that I should have coffee and brownies waiting for her in our new home. That day never arrived, she was killed in the line of duty in December 2013.

Grief, Depression & PTSD

Lost

I rise in the morning
no one to share my thoughts with.
A day seems longer than a day
when the only voice that's heard comes from inside me
searching for you.
I'm lost without your words.

I go out into the garden
no one shares my view
the garden seems empty
even with borders full of colour and never ending green.
Only one voice comes from inside me.
I'm lost without someone to share this scene.

I sit to eat my meals
no one to share my table
a place setting just for one.
When the only voice that's heard are my comments on my meal
I'm lost without the extra food for thought.

I make my way to bed, no one by my side.
The bed seems endless
I wonder where you sleep now
but I daren't speak the words
or think of you alone and cold.
Are you as lost as me?

This was the first poem I wrote after Lena's death. Four months had passed. I hadn't been able to go to her funeral, nor was I certain at that time of the circumstances of her death. The burglary had also occurred and depression along with PTSD had entered my world uninvited too, bringing with it a past I had never spoken of, having been dismissed when I attempted to report it when it occurred.

Cherry blossom

Despairing dark winter skies devour my spirit
windless, full of heavy clouds
unshifting.
I grieve for the lightest of breezes
the summer thermal
she who lifted my heart to new heights with her smile
and cherry blossom falling as pink snow drifts
in an orchard far away.

Even now more than three years after Lena's death, every cherry tree reminds me of her because she had an orchard surrounding her home. I can still picture her sitting at the foot of the cherry tree with blossom drifting by.

Pain conundrum

Which pain is worse
physical or emotional?
Which comes first?

Is it a chest pain or a rupturing heart?
Is it a headache or a breakdown?
Is it a stomach ache or am I being eaten alive?
Am I struggling to breathe or just fighting to cope?

I wish it mattered either way
but it is irrelevant
it just hurts.
Is that so hard to understand?

This was written at a point when I felt like I spoke a different language to my GP. I kept telling her my symptoms, she kept telling me I was depressed and having a 'bad grief reaction.' The only bad reaction I was having was becoming more depressed about not being listened to or taken seriously when I said I thought I was developing PTSD and needed a mental health assessment. Eventually the referral was made very grudgingly, with her describing me as 'angry and never satisfied.' That statement was used against me twice by professionals further on in my journey. The GP practice was put into special measures some months later following a Care Quality Commission inspection.

Lost without you

I left the other world behind before it swallowed me
not knowing who I was for sure, or if I could just be.

I floated round in bubbles, one for work and one for home
only slightly different, but always on my own.

The fresh start never started, I couldn't let her go
being on my own again, was unbearably low.

I'd hear a voice in a crowd, turn my head, but no
it was just my wishful thinking, a distant quiet echo.

I thought it would be simple, to let some time pass by
to find some meaning to my life and answer all the whys?

I left it all behind, I took the leap of faith
searching for that different path, as well as trusting fate.

I doubt myself so easily, there's nothing deep inside
no substance, no resilience, no sense of self resides.

By far the biggest mistake I made was to trust the health system to treat me appropriately. I was assessed for a therapeutic intervention for the first time in December 2014, by telephone, which found me to have scored insufficient points. One of the questions I was asked was 'Marital Status?' This was the day before my wedding anniversary, I couldn't answer, I was a heap on my kitchen floor. Insisting on a second assessment in March 2015 I was found to be in need. I then waited until December of that year before I was given any treatment. By that time I was struggling with night terrors, flashbacks, obsessive compulsive behaviours of checking my home, avoiding social situations and generally living in fear. The system offered me anti-depressants by the bucketful, but if I took them I couldn't work, so I did without. My work as an artist gave me structure and purpose, something I knew I needed far more than a chemical sticking plaster.

My mask

I wear my mask
it protects me from you
the one with no feelings, no words
no idea.
The one embarrassed to be heard to say
Are you ok?
Can I help in any way?

You avoid me in my mask
you run away, no time to stay.
Must dash
will call sometime
chin up.

My happy face
the one you want to see
though sadly
not me.

I don't like this poem, it is a pretty painful reminder of being avoided by 'friends' or people who knew me, who didn't know what to say to me, so they said nothing and I became invisible to them. However it is a valuable reminder that there is no right or wrong thing to say, whatever problem a person has or situation they are going through, you can just be present, be honest, but above all, be a friend.

War and peace

This is warfare, fighting not the enemy
but to find myself
shell-shocked, post-traumatic stress disordered
not from bombs and bullets
but memories in flashback.
They attack silently
the swords of psychological warfare
cutting through time, nightmare Ninjas
who engage in tactical battles on many fronts within my mind.
They confuse my strategy and harass my defenses
as they outnumber me.
Camouflaging reality
leaving trip wires for another day
as they disappear into the chaotic corners of my mind.
I am no soldier, but I fight, surrender is only a concept
a theory I don’t subscribe to, won't, can’t, never again.

Again I can’t understand where I come from
who I am, where I belong.
I have been here before, but the peace agreement is broken.
A nomad of my own mind, fantasy versus reality
was that real, or just a thought.
Did I disassociate and forget to come back to myself
or just shatter into pieces for the hell of it?
The questions and answers
they clash and rattle while I struggle
to find them and sort them into order.
Their warring distracts me
my rage and confusion hinders me
as frustration joins the list of enemies.
As I work at my task
I worry that I may miss a sighting or a clue to myself.
PTSD and OCD, they all end in D
I am merely Disordered?

Disordered for so long
it's tiring and disorientating to accept this quest
yet to refuse it is to refuse life as I want it to be.
To know there are no monsters under the bed
that the door can be unlocked
that I can close my eyes and wake without harm.
To be certain of my past; to step into myself
equipped and qualified with the truth
all of it, no matter what it is.
To know the hand that touches me is that of my lover
and she won't scare or abuse me.
She will reassure me whenever darkness falls.
My lover will be gentle and warm
she will caress my mistrustful body
stroke me into submission
kiss me softly and I welcome her warmly in return.
Order will be restored and I will have peace
peace of mind.

Living with mental illness is very tiring. Learning to manage myself as well as my conditions (PTSD, depression & anxiety panic disorder) took a lot of energy. I felt at times as though I would do two days in one day. The day everyone saw and the day I hid from view behind my mask. Things I took for granted for so long; a trip to the supermarket, getting a haircut, going to the bank, all of those things became terrifying and impossible as my PTSD grew in severity. I managed and medicated myself with my work. Eighteen hour days were my normal, I felt safer when I was working and creating as I could shelter from the triggers that brought hell to my days. At night when the nightmares disturbed and distressed me I was thankful for 'The Samaritans', who provided a human voice I could use to ground myself.

Happiness

Music: distilled, refined
crashes against this moment.
Wonder shakes its head
as I weep yesterdays across the expanse of tomorrows.
No cares or thoughts of grief, despair.
Here I sit, dissolving in waves
of yes I am here, no I fade away.
I wish I knew what to say
what to do in these times of intense emotions
but all I do is fall with the blade
cutting sorrow into tiny fragments of manageable concerns.
A snip here of morality, another of loathing
alone, lost in self-pity's welcoming arms.
Happiness, I'm not sure I can handle it.

This was written close to the point I lost hope and very nearly ended my own life. I felt as though I was a hollow shell, not living but existing in a daily pattern of terrifying nights followed by tightly guarded days, so I could try to avoid the flashbacks occurring. I was accused by one professional of 'isolating' myself, while another refused me emotional support on the grounds that re-experiencing my trauma would 'build resilience.' This was two years into my journey, I felt utterly worthless.

Precipitation

Those black clouds that form suddenly
and descend without warning.
Those dark, heavy suffocating clouds
that suck the light out of my days.
How or why they appear, cursing their victim
stalking their prey.
I often wonder whilst trapped underneath
dominating my day.

Damn those cursed clouds that need no reason
to disturb or offend.
They take hold
grasping my mind and heart
in their dirty coarse hands
sapping my energy
assaulting my sense of self
invoking bodily responses that scare
making me question everything
searching for jigsaw pieces of the sun to banish the clouds.

But today, I fear I must wait for a wind of change
to blow these clouds away.
Should I give in and just let it rain
to wash them away?

Alone & writing

Alone, thinking and writing
leaking thoughts.
A task which allows me to ask
questions, deep and brave
seeking the answers I crave.

There is no gain
thoughts like rain
pour on the paper
the drain.
Gone, before I can catch them
snatching at the air
desperate to share.
Each piece of knowledge never lingers
slips through my fingers.

My thirst is never sated
just more questions created
just a sliver, a minute quiver
catches on my pen
saved and written for posterity.

I often had a head full of thoughts and while they were in my head they could run amok aided and abetted by depression, anxiety, PTSD or any other human condition. What writing did for me was to nail down those words, it stopped them running wild and reinventing their meanings in my mind. Once committed to the page, there could be no doubt to their meaning. Looking back now in June 2017, it gives me a sense of how far I have travelled. I would commend writing to anyone. Record your journey, spelling and grammar are not important, witnessing your own experience is.

Life cycles

We have as long as fate dictates
just that long and no more
like a washing machine programmed
for so many washes until we're scaled up
don't work any more.

Some of us work on a delicates wash
take it easy, stay cool, live with care.
Others heat up to boiling point
live life in the fast wash, for a dare.
Main wash stay down the middle
never deviate left or right
whatever gets them through the night.

Pre-wash are different, take extra time.
On programme one, they can't quite get going
push the next button, move on.
Economy, always a struggle
trying to make ends meet
in hot water, tangled, a muddle
all washed up, out on the street.

Many bypass every wash setting, lose the plot
get in a spin, faster and faster.
Quick wash, they never catch up
or change the state they are in.

Some have it all sorted, wash, dry, ironed the lot!
Confident, laid back, dried flat.
Freshly laundered, hung in a gale.
Should we envy or tell ourselves
they sometimes get lime scale?
But some troubled souls
lose their bearings
asking what does this life mean?
When family and friends check the label
they find, too late
it says Special Needs - dry clean.

Finding my voice

A shaft of moonlight illuminates the night in front of me
the glowing fire crackles and stutters behind me
the world slumbers quietly around me.
No other sound invades this solitary place
until the pen cuts through the surface of the paper
breaking the silence
tattooing my unconscious upon the page.
The words assemble covertly
before plotting their escape down the pen
the ink dances rebelliously in swathes
while my mouth remains pathetically silent.

Caught within my mouth
so many things to say but the words are jumbled
swilling around like washing
awaiting the stains of shame to dissolve and disperse.
The ink is less easily shamed or contained
it races for freedom, pouring from the nib
blowing contemptuous raspberries
and hissing 'fuck you' at my dumb lips.

It demands the paper soak up every drop
in the form and meaning that has waited for this moment.
It rejoices in making its own mark
proclaiming itself the blood of thought.
It colours and commands every fibre that it touches
giving meaning and breathing life into the page
once so lifeless, so quiet.

The words squawk and screech like baby birds
breaking free from their eggs.
They fledge quickly and learn to fly
lifting themselves on token breezes of my breath
flying on thermals of meaning in front of my eyes.
They circle my head and rest there for a while
before leaving to forge a path through the darkness
for my voice to find.

This poem marked a shift in me. I wrote it shortly after I had made the very definite decision not to end my life, a choice I made standing on a beach. I drew a physical line in the sand. I understood if I stepped over that line I had to find myself again and stand up to the disempowerment and attitudes of the services who were supposed to be there to aid my recovery.

I have found my voice now and my sense of self and I won't lose it or allow it to be taken or silenced again.

In the shadows of PTSD

Dark noises in the shadows scream
between the worlds of sleep and dreams.
They merge and morph upon the dark water edge of consciousness
where fear commences and hope is worn by nightly tides of terror
The bed that is no longer restful, but instead the harbour of dread.

I wake on other shores, cowering in corners
moved by invisible tides and monsters
gargoyles gnawing on my bones.
A helping hand grotesquely melts, burning mine
I recoil, shocked, gasping, pulse racing
I search for the labyrinth exit.

A cold wall or floor my doorway to reality
something, anything to tell me it's over.
My eyes search for the sky, clouds never so welcome
stars never so blessed.
A gulp of cold water and a grounding script
then I am nightmare free
until sleep beckons me back, tomorrow.

If anyone asked me which part of the last three years was the most difficult and the most intrusive, it is without doubt the nightmares. I would regularly wake up in different parts of my home with no recollection of how I got there, corners of rooms, behind doors, often injured in the process, presumably by fighting imaginary attackers. I also shouted in my sleep, so the idea of going away for a break or holiday was unthinkable. I had been experiencing this on a regular basis since August 2015. The only help I was offered prior to my EMDR therapy was sleeping pills, hard to believe but true. I refused them.

Footprints

Tiny grains of sand washed upon the shore
brought before me on tides of constant change
history shifting in my footprints.

This is one of my favourite poems, it's very small but says so much. The message for me is that some things change constantly, some have to be changed.

Another world

Dawn dances on the canal
breakfasting to the sounds of morning arrive outside
while those I love sleep inside.
All moments passed stand still
the sky, the air, the space above our heads
embraces me, lifts me, carries me
to show me a world long imagined.
I am home.

I wrote this in the summer of 2016. I was on a narrowboat in Yorkshire with my best friend, her daughter (my God daughter) and Lena's aunt, Galina. It was the first time we had all been together since Lena's death and the first time I felt truly safe and at peace.

In purple

A gold sky shines beneath a wreck of cloud
the pale silver sand is cooled by the sea
miles away rise the cliffs of fantasy
naked and treeless, dark as starless light.

The roll of the ocean's music is loud
you sit on the grass in purple, head bowed
a small bundle in the dusk, curled up tight
speechless in the mazes of prophecy
spellbound by twisting colours of fancy.

I feel you in me, radiant and white
your lovely face is lit with lilac light.

It was during the time in Yorkshire I had my first dream of Lena that wasn't nightmarish in any way. It is still the only one at the time of writing in June 2017, but I have the image and I have this poem and they are enough to remind me of how things can be.

Staying solid

When things are this way
disappointing
it is important to stay solid.

Compact
like particles at minus forty
do not subscribe to chaos.

Contract
not contort
collide as little as possible.

When it is time
to break out of the icy prison
something will tell me.

This represents the time I knew I had to keep myself together and wait for my EMDR assessment and hope that I would be given the treatment. I received the news on August 23rd 2016 to say that was going to happen, everything I had held together spilled out. I cried for what felt like hours, the sheer relief of knowing recovery was finally a possibility.

Sunflower

Just a few months ago
a field of sunflowers held
their golden faces high
worshipping the sun's rays
heat incubating their seed heads.
Today nothing but dark ochre
bent stems staring down at frozen soil.

Ravens gather, picking at ripened seeds
filling their greedy bellies
before flying off to search for lost souls
crackling with defiance and laughing
at mortal kindness.

Each season takes their turn
winters drab colours quietly whisper summer is nigh.
I will wait patiently like the sunflower for the summer's heat
to dance upon my lawn.

I did wait patiently and I can hold my head up once more.

My body

My body remembers yours
it remembers your head on my chest
smiling, with your eyes closed
as you listened to my heart '*play the drums.*'

It remembers you stroking my head
as I read to you, your favourite pleasure
'a bath isn't a bath without your words.'

It remembers your gentle smile as you held my head in your hands
by my ears like Snow White with Dopey
as if I cared when you kissed me.
Even you didn't have words for those moments.

I miss holding your hand
sometimes it felt quite small and I took care of you.
Other times you led me, away from wolves and bears
or used me as bait for hungry catfish
but I still miss holding your hand.

My body misses you.
I miss you.

When I finally entered EMDR treatment in October 2016 with a caring, compassionate doctor, feeling safe brought mixed blessings. While it was comforting to have someone who cared about me and my recovery, my body previously detached from the trauma began to re-connect with it. I began to re-experience the trauma physically. Flashbacks came complete with smells, sounds and physical pain. At their worst they rooted me to the spot, unable to move or speak as I would feel a knife at my throat, or worse. I did write about it, but I also burned it, as those memories have no place in my journey now. Instead I chose to write about what my body remembered when I was with Lena, the fun stuff, the caring stuff, the things that made her special. This poem is the antidote to all of the toxic and uninvited intrusions I endured.

Last night

Last night's silver flood of light laps
against my memory's edge.
Liquid touches whose insistence undid
all my resistance, made collapse
my courage to refuse, to lapse
back in the blink of an eyelid.

I stare through the haze of daybreak
seeking the one that I missed
in the golden maze of the mist.
My eyes go white, lost in the ache of longing
I stand by the lake
on the shore where you kissed my wrist.

The unending sky is cloudless
the water a smooth blue mirror.
The bliss I wished does not recur
no trace or whisper comes to bless
the gift you unhitched from your dress
a spray of uncrushed lavender.

Grieving is different for everyone. I have done most of mine through writing and speaking to Lena. I refuse to be ashamed of speaking to her spirit. I read to her on her birthday and our wedding anniversary as that was what she always asked for. She was the first person to hear this book , on what would have been her 50th birthday.

The landlocked mermaid

The lake is still,
fish swim silently like ghosts
the water lilies undisturbed
await the artist's impression
as insects skip across the water.

I swim and reflect upon my many years within this lake
it is not in my nature to dwell in the past
but like the storms of oceans long gone
I am wild and forgetful.

You may see me, a flash of silver in the moonlight
but as quick as you see me, I am gone
to depths you cannot fathom
leaving only a whisper in my wake
from the landlocked mermaid with a tale to tell.

This is my metaphor for feeling trapped, disassociating at the worst points and escaping to be with the mermaids. I don't do it now, it is no longer necessary. I like this poem and I've always liked mermaids.

Echo of a shadow

Daze dance of flowing moment here
beyond the dream of time
where moving magic light is clear
and solitude is mine.

There is a sadness in their drift
from time to age gone by
where springtime was a welcome shift
and loved ones wouldn't die.

But in the dance the leaves just fade
and echoes lift my soul
so pictures in my mind are made
most lovingly quite whole.

I thought that I had finished writing about my grief and then I began my EMDR treatment. For the first time someone acknowledged my loss and validated my process as being a healthy one. My spiritual beliefs were not criticised as they previously had been and I no longer felt the need to censor or guard what I said, because here was a person I could trust not to judge and criticise but to listen and empathise.

Magical currents

Oceanographic splashes sweet delight
as I open this body's seas
seize magical currents of ecological fancies
and laugh chemistry across cold foresight
swim in violent torrents.

Ancient souls gather visions
as tides ebb and flow smoothly.
Calmly I reach for the essences of night
stars sail the sky with gentle ease
journeys of time's merchants.
Smiles dance love in nature's medleys
while wild passion's structure is set alight
here there's only brilliance.

Crescents roll through minds canyons
Relaxation sighs loudly.
Deep silence emerges with cool grace
space winks as water caresses this face.

I wrote this as the antidote to a series of disturbing nightmares, which challenged my reality of had I woken or was I still within the nightmare? The final part of the nightmare was that I thought I was awake sitting on the edge of the bed, so stood up to go and get a drink of water. In that moment a sea of epic proportions rose up towards me and I woke up on the bedroom floor, panic stricken. When I had gathered myself I went to the bathroom to splash cold water on my face to test if I was awake or not. I was thankfully. This poem turns that nightmare into the act of washing my face, making it bearable and removes the terror I felt.

Risk assessment
Trigger Warning: elements of this poem may cause alarm

I drive
fearing only
(in my ultra safe Volvo)
that I may lack concentration.
If this occurs I can rely on:
side impact protection
airbags
seat belts
and if all else fails
legendary tank like qualities
(the car that is)
not me.

Driving for the most part keeps me safe
away from:

1. the men who attack
2. the noise that pierces my personal space
3. and likewise the general public

(who can be a danger to themselves, let alone me).

The latest email from my Amygdala declares
the current threat level as 'Severe' and reads:
Warning!
Dear Victim
You must be hyper vigilant at all times.
Avoid the following as they/it will do you severe harm:
men
drunk men
men laughing
men shouting
men with beards
men with tattoos
men with beards and tattoos
or any combination of the above.
The smell of alcohol
pint glasses of beer
also cans of.

Smirnoff and whisky in glasses or bottles
are especially dangerous
as are cigarettes
cigarette smoke
and cigarette butts.
Newspapers are not to be underestimated
fake news is bad enough
but dirty crumpled pages
can choke and silence when applied orally
and chips
the smell of chips will make you sick.

Knives, shiny, sharp, silver ones (no serrations).
Green garden twine
white washing line
brown garden shed
cracked mugs in dirty sinks
angry voices
shouting
dark places
enclosed spaces
multi-storey parking places
unexpected noises that startle
(alarms cause alarm)
and bodily contact
maintain a 5 metre safety zone
absolutely no hugging strangers
(friends must be thoroughly vetted).

Failure to comply with this directive
will result in sanctions:
I may steal your voice
your breath
your sense of self.
I will make you sweat
(and that is something else to be avoided)
I will flood you with adrenaline
inducing panic.
You will become immobile.
You will have flashbacks.

Your will want the world to swallow you up
but it won't, ha ha
emotional terrorism
my speciality!

Hey where have you gone?
I'm still talking!

You have to listen to me, I am your primeval response

Who said you could disassociate?
Come back!

That's not fair

Your frontal lobe doesn't love you like I do.

The amygdala is the brain's emotional processor and controls how we react to external stimuli. The frontal lobe is where logic is processed. The poem represents how my processor is stuck in warnings and how many messages it was sending each time I went out and how any one of those things could potentially result in the responses I have listed as 'sanctions.' The logical part of me knows I shouldn't be afraid of certain things, but the amygdala is much stronger and cannot be ignored. EMDR (eye movement, desensitization and reprogramming) therapy is about re-programming this response so it is no longer based on historical trauma. I wrote this poem in June 2017, as the result of a request from The Good Doctor, who asked me if I could write a poem about how I felt when I had to venture outside my safe zones. This poem became part of my treatment.

Fear of drowning

I used to visit the sea
drawn to it to sit for hours
watching the waves drag the shingle from the shore
snatched into the icy waters against its will.

I used to feel like shingle
a small piece of stone
insignificant
at the mercy of the sea, waiting to drown.

I used to wake at night
sweating, breathing distorted
as the sea dragged me from my beach
thrashing about and helpless
but no more.

I looked today upon the sea
it was calm and gently lapping
I pictured myself, serene and floating
in control of the water
in control of my destiny.

Embracing the water
not fearing it.
Drowning only my fears.

Sky poem

Alone with my kite in the serene evening moonlight
standing in the cool wet sand my toes dive deep like hungry roots
anchoring me in centuries of sediment.
Hearing only the sea breathe and seals sing
I feel the lines in my hands and tune myself to the winds breath.

She is light and playful on the back of my neck
like a lover whispering their intention.
I bring my outstretched my hands towards me
adding tension to the lines.

I tease her with the top edge of my kite
like a fisherman casting a fly on the river.
She grasps it playfully and lifts it gently skywards
before we tie the earth and sky together
with only the stars as our audience.

Anyone who knows me will tell you I love kites. I love making them and flying them. When I need to 'be', or free myself, I go to Holy Island at night. I walk out on to the sand and I launch a kite, flying it in the dark totally by feeling, tuning myself to the elements. There is no feeling quite like it and when I leave I am centred, focussed and ready for the next challenge.

The Good Doctor, the tree and me

When I arrived I was like the tree I see
through the window of the office of The Good Doctor.
There the tree stood, alone, frozen, leafless in the midst of winter.
She was not free, she was confined, fenced in.
No birds sat on her branches to sing
no children to climb or swing.
Was she the tree that only I see?

I sit in the blue chair, by the white board
while The Good Doctor, a gardener of the mind
explores my PTSD fears and black memories
listening gently to my experience
in the third winter of my discontent.

She, The Good Doctor, is reassuringly calm
benevolent.
I am not.
I am filled with terror and dread
I need the sky to ground me
as I unearth the past, buried deep within.
It breaks free like a rabid animal
mauling me day and night
stealing my breath, forcing nightmare scenarios.

My weekly visit to the blue chair by the white board
at the end of the long grey corridor of salvation
with The Good Doctor.
She teaches me mantras of safety
'I am vulnerable'
'That was then, this is now'
installed through my blue eyes
by moving lights on the black box
and pulsing silver buttons in my white sweating hands.
This is EMDR.

The rabid dogs of trauma are unleashed
to see where they may lead me
Have we tamed them?
No, they bite and tear at me.
My mantras are no match
I recoil into the present
searching for the sky and my tree
with The Good Doctor reminding me I am safe.

My life is drawn with a black line on the white board
by The Good Doctor
above is happy, below is not.
Fifty three years condensed in three weekly visits
to give respite from the rabid dogs
and search for lurking beliefs.

Bolstered by belief
with courage held close
the dogs again unleashed
as are my mantras, arming me against their teeth.
I'm not yet safe, but nor am I re-torn
they may snap and snarl
but I will tame them one day.

The sky is blue now, it is spring.
The tree is growing, as am I.
The tree has leaves, I have hope
The tree has blossom, I have belief
The Good Doctor smiles, so do I.

I chose to make this poem the last one in the book because it is a story of hope, my story of hope, restored to me by a skilled and compassionate doctor. I now believe I am on the path to recovery and I will do whatever I need to do to stay on that path because with hope comes belief, with belief comes courage and with courage comes strength.

Biography

I was born in 1964 and have always been innately creative. In previous careers I worked with children and young people in education and social care settings, built countless gardens and travelled the world, experiencing different cultures and photographing them. I began working as an artist in 2012.
Since Lena's death I focussed my energy into building Happy Planet Creative Arts CIC, a social enterprise, based in Whitley Bay. This gave me the structure and purpose I knew I needed when everything felt like it was falling apart.
Happy Planet now encourages others to embrace and explore their creativity to aid their wellbeing, as well as showcasing and selling other local artists' work.
This is my first published collection of poetry. I have begun writing my memoir, but I may well paint a few more poems before that is finished.
If you would like to know more about Happy Planet you can visit my website at **www.happyplanetcreativearts.org.uk** alternatively you would be welcome to visit the gallery in person.

Gail Curry
June 2017

Acknowledgements

My journey could have been very different if it were not for certain organisations and individuals. I therefore offer my heartfelt gratitude to all of the following:
The Samaritans were always there for me when I needed to hear another human voice at the most inhospitable times.
Jo Copeland of North East NHS Independent Complaints Advocacy, who guided me through the shark-infested waters of the local NHS Trusts complaints procedures.
Angie Stanger-Leathes of Limelight Classic Productions, who very kindly guided me through the technicalities of self-publishing and took care of those I could not.
My friends, of the very best kind, Anya Klovochesky, Kate Bromwich-Alexandra, Maureen Sanderson, Elaine Maughan and Frances Storey, who listened and cushioned my journey until I met the right person to light the way.
Elaine Cusack, my excellent friend, sounding board and editor, without whom you would not be reading this book.
And finally, Dr Renuka Arjundas, 'The Good Doctor', compassionate, skilled and generous, who returned hope to me when it was lost and lit my path to recovery. I shall miss her and her tree.

While I did not receive the support of Rape Crisis Tyneside & Northumberland, I have no hesitation in making them the beneficiary of my book. I know they make an immeasurable difference to many other women's and girls' lives and must continue to do so while our bodies and rights are not respected.

Rape Crisis Tyneside and Northumberland
Charity No: 1138149

The charity was established in 1978 and was originally known as Tyneside Rape Crisis Centre. The charity name was changed in 2010 when the Northumberland pilot project became formally part of the main charity's work.The areas we cover are: Gateshead, Newcastle upon Tyne, North Tyneside, Northumberland and South Tyneside.We are the longest continuously running Rape Crisis service in the UK, and are looking ahead at celebrating our 40th year in 2018.

Who we help and support
The charity has two key objectives:
1) to support girls and women aged 13 and over who have experienced any form of sexual violence at any time in their lives.
2) to educate and raise awareness about the impact of sexual violence.

The charity offers a range of direct services to support survivors of sexual violence such as counselling, email support, groupwork, helpline service and practical/emotional support.
Education and raising awareness work is undertaken by Community engagement and development workers.

We are a growing organisation, having expanded in recent years to develop our direct services and expand community and public engagement. We have increased our media profile and undertake a range of fundraising activities throughout the year to increase awareness of our service and also raise funds to support our work and activities.

0191 222 0272
enquiries@rctn.org.uk
www.rctn.org.uk

Helpline & Email Support
0800 035 2794 or emailsupport@rctn.org.uk
Tuesday, Wednesday & Thursday 6pm – 8.30pm
and Friday 11am - 2pm

Helpful mental health support

If you're experiencing mental health problems or need support, here are some of the organisations you can go to for help.

Samaritans

Telephone: 116 123 (24 hours a day, free to call)
Email: jo@samaritans.org
Website: www.samaritans.org

Provides confidential, non-judgmental emotional support for people experiencing feelings of distress or despair, including those that could lead to suicide. You can phone, email, write a letter or in most cases talk to someone face to face.

Mind Infoline

Telephone: 0300 123 3393 (9am-6pm Monday to Friday)
Email: info@mind.org.uk
Web site: www.mind.org.uk/help/advice_lines

Mind provides confidential mental health information services.

With support and understanding, Mind enables people to make informed choices. The Infoline gives information on types of mental distress, where to get help, drug treatments, alternative therapies and advocacy. Mind has around 140 local Minds providing local mental health services.

The Mix

Telephone: 0808 808 4994(11am-11pm, free to call)
Email: Helpline email form
Website: www.themix.org.uk/get-support

The Mix provides judgement-free information and support to young people aged 13-25 on a range of issues including mental health problems. Young people can access the The Mix's support via phone, email, peer to peer and counselling services.

75900657R00041

Made in the USA
Columbia, SC
29 August 2017